From here to there

Managing change in third sector organisations

Contents

Chapter 1: Managing change in third sector organisations

"You'll make mistakes along the way. Accept them. Move on. You'll still get where you're going."
Project contributor

1.1 Why a guide on change?

Whether they want to or not, all third sector organisations (TSOs)[1] have to deal with change.

Organisational change can come from within your organisation. This could be in response to a review of your performance or strategy, a change in key personnel, or ideas on how to improve the organisation from your staff, volunteers or users.

Change can also be forced on your organisation from outside. Your organisation may need to change to respond to new legislation, social change or new technology. It may want to expand to take advantage of new funding opportunities.

As a manager, trustee or chief executive of a TSO, coping with change is an integral part of your everyday work. However, it's worth taking some time to understand and manage change to ensure you steer your organisation to a desired future. Planning for and managing change will also help you minimise any negative impacts that upheaval can have on your users, staff, trustees and organisational culture.

This guide will help you consider the common and important issues that face all TSOs when planning for and managing significant changes to their organisation.

If you're interested in reading more about change management, we've put together a list of resources which you can view and download from our website **www.performancehub.org.uk/managingchange**

1.2 What's distinctive about the third sector and managing change?

Organisations in all sectors face some common challenges when undergoing change. However, third sector managers may face some unique challenges, including stakeholders with very different motivations to those in the private or public sectors and the need to manage short-term funding cycles. This guide acknowledges the particular challenges and benefits of working with people in the third sector.

Third sector organisations have a unique and complex mix of stakeholders. In particular, managers may have a limited formal influence over volunteers and trustees, who give their time on an unpaid basis. Similarly, independent charities that are part of federated organisations can use their autonomy to side-step the plans and priorities of 'head office'. Driving change with people who can readily choose whether or not to 'get with the programme' requires a more inclusive, values-based approach. Managers may need to appeal to and manage stakeholder passions, emotions, commitment or attachment to people, places or causes.

Three-year funding cycles mean that third sector organisations often rapidly expand or contract in size. Data from the NCVO Almanac[2] suggests that it is not uncommon for TSOs to double or half their income over three years. Such rapid growth or shrinkage presents a considerable challenge for TSOs.

Finally, changing relationships with the public sector, coupled with increased competition for grant funding, has driven many TSOs to re-think what they do and how they do it, in order to meet their aims.

1.3 Leading change successfully

How change is led will profoundly influence whether it is successful or not. The process of leading change involves making subtle judgements about what approach to take with people, when to drive change forward or slow the pace. There is no single approach to leading change successfully, as every situation is different. Above all, it's about achieving a balance between having a clear but flexible plan; setting ambitious but realistic targets; allowing input and debate, whilst being decisive when necessary.

This guide will help you to identify the kind of change taking place in your organisation, consider different approaches to managing change, and use practical techniques and tools to help people deal with change.

1.4 How to use the guide

This guide is aimed at third sector leaders and managers, who may be involved in leading change. It is primarily aimed at those in established organisations with paid staff and clear management roles, but it may also contain useful ideas for very small organisations or informal groups.

This guide explores the issues to be considered during change, and the management strategies that can make change succeed or fail. It offers guidance, encouragement and an opportunity to reflect on your organisation.

It is not a 'how to' guide to change management. Other resources can help with this, including the companion reference guide on change management resources on the Performance Hub website at **www.performancehub.org.uk/managingchange** The guide might be used alongside your regular planning cycles or management systems while the organisation is embarking upon change.

This guide builds on established management theory and thinking from across sectors and countries. It also contains direct learning from third sector leaders and managers who attended a one-day workshop on managing change, or submitted case studies about their real-life change experiences.

1.5 Words of advice on change

Practitioners in the sector were asked what advice they would offer to readers of the guide, based on their own experiences of managing change. Here are just a few of their comments. Further quotes from them are dispersed throughout the guide.

"You're not alone. It's a team effort - you can't manage everything single-handedly."

"Communicate constantly, consistently and to a plan."

"Use your judgement. Trust your instincts."

"Take a deep breath and make one step at a time."

1 charities, voluntary organisations, community groups and social enterprises

2 Kane D, Reichart O and Wilding K *The UK Voluntary Sector Almanac: The State of the Sector 2007* (London, NCVO, 2007)

Chapter 2: What kind of change are you dealing with?

> ***"Take time out to look at the big picture of the change you're facing - think about the different elements you need to address."***
>
> **Project contributor**

In order to manage change, the first step is to be clear about what kind of change you're dealing with. This will help you to understand it and prepare an appropriate response.

There are three main factors to consider:

1. **the reason:** Why is a change needed?
2. **the scale:** How far reaching/fundamental is the change?
3. **the urgency and importance:** How urgent and/or important is this change?

2.1 *Reasons for change*

Understanding the reason for change can help you identify what results need to be achieved and who needs to be involved.

Change can result from forces from within or outside the organisation. They can also be planned or unplanned.

Change from within

Internal processes may highlight the need for a change. For example, a strategic review could lead to changing your vision, mission or ways of working. Alternatively, assessing your progress against plans and targets or comparing performance and practice with other organisations or against established quality standards may highlight the need to improve or develop aspects of the organisation's activities. Frontline staff or users may suggest how you could improve your products or services.

Staff often find new and better ways of doing things over time. Sometimes small changes in day-to-day activities can have a big impact on people's experience of the workplace or an organisation's services. This is a form of learning-based change.

The challenge for an organisation is to identify this kind of learning and replicate it across the organisation. Think about the different ways your organisation captures learning and good practice. When a good idea comes up, what do you do about it?

Sharing and embedding emerging good practice across the organisation will involve managing changes in existing practice.

Change from outside the organisation

Externally, funders and commissioners can make demands that require a review or reshaping of activities. Change to legislation, technology, society or the economy can create new challenges that must be addressed.

Planned change

Planned changes are usually the result of changes that are identified internally. They could result from an organisation's strategic or business planning processes, an evaluation, a benchmarking exercise or working towards a quality standard.

Unplanned change

Some changes need to take place to respond to unexpected events. These are often external events, like those mentioned above, but they can also come from within, such as changes in key personnel.

> ***Case study: Change from within***
>
> **Aaina Asian Women's Group** carried out a full organisational review that considered the evolving needs of local people and what the organisation could offer to service users and partners. It carried out an internal audit alongside a consultation and evaluation with service users. It also reviewed local regeneration funding and strategies. The organisation is now focusing on five areas of delivery, and is developing two social enterprises to generate income to fund core costs and salary costs alongside commissioned and funded projects.

Unplanned events which would make it difficult or even impossible for your organisation to carry out its day-to-day activities can be described as crises. A crisis could be a fire or flooding in the office, illness of key members of staff or an IT system failure.

A good risk management strategy will help you to anticipate some of these unplanned events and to consider possible responses.[3] Likewise, it's a good idea to have a crisis management strategy in place, which sets out how your organisation would get back on track in the event of any of the scenarios mentioned above.[4]

2.2 Scale of change

Will this change affect the whole organisation, or just one team, office or department? Is the change fundamental, does it just skim the surface, or somewhere in between?

Being clear about the scale of change can help you identify what resources you need and the timescales that may be involved.

Organisation-wide change

This is where change affects every part of the organisation, such as a major restructuring or a culture change. This kind of change is likely to require significant planning and management.

Sub-system change

This is change that affects only a particular part of the organisation, such as introducing a new service or

> ***Example: Learning leads to change***
>
> A charity supporting people through substance abuse manages street support teams from a head office.
>
> Working practices like client outreach and support sessions are designed and defined by a support services team at head office.
>
> Those with the direct experience of working with clients, the street support teams, know from experience that clients will respond more positively if support sessions are planned in certain locations at different times from those suggested by head office.
>
> The street support team leaders meet with the support services team at head office on a regular basis. At their next review meeting the street support team leaders explain their experiences of engaging clients and propose a new support plan and schedule for client outreach.
>
> The head office team understands the value of the new approach and feeds the suggestion back to the senior management team. At the next business plan review, senior managers agree to implement the new support plan across the organisation.

3 Leitch M 'Managing risk and uncertainty' *Achieve More magazine*, issue 8 (London, Performance Hub, 2007) **www.performancehub.org.uk/achievemore8** and **www.internalcontrolsdesign.co.uk**

4 Business Links website **www.businesslink.gov.uk**

ending a project, reorganising a department or function, or implementing a new system or process.

This kind of change may require management only in the part of the organisation affected by it. However, changes to one part of the organisation will often mean changes to other parts too. Even when a change only affects a few people, you should communicate what the change is and the reasons behind it right across your organisation. A lack of information often leads to people inventing their own fantasies about what's going on ("It'll be us next!"), which can be quite unsettling.

Transformational change (also known as radical, fundamental or quantum change)

This is where change fundamentally alters the whole organisation in one massive transition. Some examples would be changing an organisation's structure and culture from the traditional top-down, hierarchical structure to a flatter structure with number of self-directing teams, or changing from a traditional charity to a social enterprise based on entrepreneurial beliefs and attitudes.

This kind of change is typically a response to a major opportunity or threat facing the organisation, and is led by the trustees and senior management.

Developmental change

This is change that builds and improves on current activities and ways of working, such as modifying your current services, or expanding the number or type of users you support.

2.3 Urgency and importance of change

Thinking about how urgent and important the change is can help you prioritise it in relation to other development within the organisation. It should also help you plan an appropriate timeframe to implement the change. Some changes will need to be implemented as quickly as possible, others will benefit from a more gradual approach.

Incremental or emergent change

This is change that happens gradually, in a step-by-step or continual way. It may result from continuous improvement or organisational development activities. The change may be led formally within the organisation or it may take place informally, as a grassroots drive to improve, which is then taken up by management. Some examples might be re-shaping services in response to user or frontline worker feedback or introducing a quality assurance system.

Remedial change

This is change that is intended to resolve or remedy a problem such as introducing new financial controls and processes or introducing performance measures and indicators.

It's typically focused and urgent because it addresses a current, major problem. It is often easier to see the success of this kind of change because it's clear whether the situation is resolved or not.

"Remember why you're changing."
Project contributor

Case study: Transformational change

Groundwork Black Country grew significantly following the award of a large single regeneration budget (SRB) delivery programme in 1998. This growth was sustained until 2005 when the scaling back of the SRB programme reduced funding and meant the organisation could not continue with the same level of activity. Despite making some small adjustments, by the start of 2006 it was apparent that the organisation needed to make some fundamental changes in order to survive.

In April 2006, a new chair was elected after the departure of the previous executive director. The deputy director was appointed to act up to oversee the organisation's plan for change. The approach to change was radical and included:

- reshaping the management structure to manage staff by themes not geographical units
- redefining the products and services
- making 25 compulsory redundancies
- moving out of four sites and relocating into two sites
- three resignations and three new additions to the board.

The biggest challenge facing Groundwork Black Country was to turn around some large financial deficits incurred over the previous two financial years. Part of meeting this challenge involved reducing some staff teams and interviewing staff for redefined posts. Making redundancies was by far the hardest part of change. It had a huge effect on those directly affected as well as other staff around the organisation. Groundwork provided one-on-one support to the staff made redundant, helping them search for new jobs and ensuring they had up-to-date CVs. No appeals or tribunals were received following the redundancy process.

Chapter 3: Choosing an approach to managing change

This section considers a number of different approaches to managing change. To decide on your own approach, you will need to consider the:

1. type of change facing the organisation (explored in chapter 2)
2. what you want the change to achieve (vision and aims)
3. culture of the organisation
4. current leadership or management style within the organisation.

This part of the guide also suggests some personal strategies for people leading or managing change.

3.1 Understanding organisational culture

Understanding your organisation's culture can help you choose the appropriate approach to managing change and identify suitable activities to support change. Current culture may support a planned change, or it could stand in the way of it.

Culture is commonly seen as 'the way things happen' in an organisation – especially the particular ways that people normally behave and the broad, generally sub-conscious assumptions they hold about 'the ways things are in this organisation'.

Culture is reflected in and influenced by the way people interact with each other, and is always evolving. The dominant culture is shaped by leaders and senior managers, organisational values and structures, and key processes – either consciously or sub-consciously.

Sub-cultures can form in parts of the organisation to create behaviours and beliefs unique to a small group of people.

When managing change, you should consider the organisation's culture. In a culture when people are accustomed to being treated in a democratic style and actively involved in decision-making, a highly directive change strategy where decisions are made by senior management and handed down for immediate action, is unlikely to win much support. Similarly a stakeholder-defined strategy using a highly participative, democratic approach will appear alien and unsettling if the organisation is historically hierarchical and staff expect senior managers to make and communicate decisions for them to implement.

Sometimes organisational cultures themselves need to change to enable an organisation to achieve its goals. For example, a grant-funded voluntary organisation may need a fundamental shift in culture (attitudes, beliefs, motivators, processes) in order to become a successful social enterprise.

"Whether people's personal values match the organisation's values will affect their reaction to change."
Project contributor

Exercise: ***Cultural webs***[5]

A cultural web is a tool to help people think about what their organisation is like at the moment, how they want it to be, and how the two compare. Producing cultural webs can help you identify what you want to change, and this is particularly useful if you are unsure about the root cause of some of the issues you want to address. The web contains six elements:

1. **Stories** that are told in or about the organisation
2. **Symbols** that appear in the organisation
3. **Power structures** within the organisation
4. **Organisational structures**
5. **Control systems** in the organisation
6. **Rituals and routines** in the organisation.

Figure 1: The Cultural Web[6]

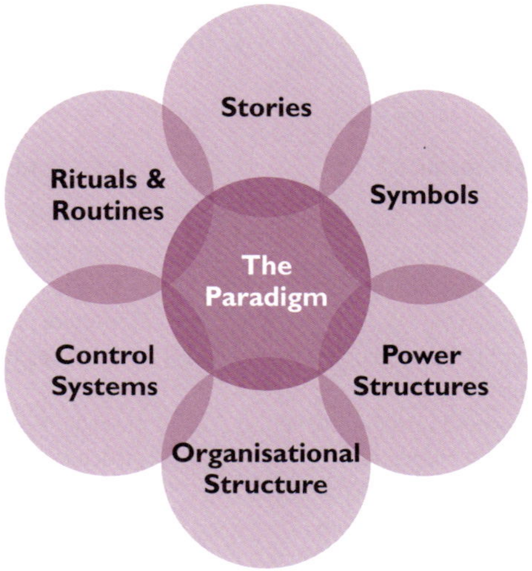

Using the cultural web

Cultural webs can be produced in interactive workshops, to help engage stakeholders in identifying the need for change. They enable people to explore and understand the culture of an organisation. They can reveal different perceptions and understanding in different parts of the organisation.

If you decide to use cultural webs in a workshop, start with the concept of the web and what it aims to achieve. Ask workshop participants to discuss and identify the things they consider indicate the different elements of the organisation's culture.

Once people have identified these indicators, ask them to think about how they would *like* each element of their organisation's culture to be. You might want to provide some parameters to this so that people think about what is realistic and achievable.

As they do this, a new cultural web is produced, one with many points of contrast to the web showing the present state of the organisation.

The table opposite gives examples of things that people might identify about their organisation's culture.

Cultural webs showing present and future can be used as the basis for planning areas of change. The participation of a range of people in producing these webs helps build support for any proposed change.

5 Adapted from Johnson G 'Mapping and re-mapping organisational culture: a local government example' in Johnson G and Scholes K (eds) *Exploring Public Sector Strategy* (London, Prentice Hall, 2001)

6 www.mindtools.com

Web element	***Indicators of current culture***	***Indicators of future culture***
Stories	→ 'Jean on reception will look after you' → 'We always do what the Council tells us'	→ 'We know where we're going' → 'You get listened to here'
Symbols	→ Kitchen/staff room is messy and worn → Chair of trustees allocated parking space → Formal dress code	→ Kitchen/staff room refitted and modern → Parking based on need → No dress code
Power	Decisions are made by: → Senior management team → Trustee board → Union rep and staff reps	→ Responsibility is devolved → Empowerment → Peer advisory team
Organisational structures	→ Hierarchical → Team silos → Patriarchal	→ Flat structure → Cross-team working → Responsive decision-making
Control systems	→ Delivery plan → Budgets → Contract compliance	→ Business plans → Financial controls → Stakeholder audit
Rituals and routines	→ Weekly team meetings → Only the senior management team meet the trustees → Sending 'everyone' emails about social events	→ Biannual all staff meetings → Trustees mentor staff → Social secretary posts social events on an extranet

Case study:
Changing culture to develop the organisation

B Arts, an arts organisation based in Stoke-on-Trent, wanted to become a more diverse organisation to better reflect and serve its local area. B Arts looked for people to join the organisation from its beneficiary communities. For its newly expanded team to work together effectively however, B Arts recognised it had to work differently.

Firstly it learned to respect and celebrate Islamic holidays. Communication methods changed because of language gaps. Face-to-face discussion and text messaging now helps to ensure communication meets everyone's needs. Colleagues are encouraged to take time to sit and eat lunch together – making the time more sociable and relaxing.

3.2 *Changing organisational culture*

Changing culture is difficult and happens slowly. Some writers on change believe that people "act themselves into new ways of thinking", rather than "thinking themselves into new ways of acting". In other words, to change a culture you should first need to change people's behaviour, which affects their attitudes and beliefs, not the other way around.

Leaders and managers often try to change or align organisational values – the fundamental guiding principles the organisation works to. However, often it's not people's values that need to change, it's their beliefs. Beliefs in who you can trust, or what behaviour will be rewarded or punished, are influenced by training, daily experience or what people say and hear. Beliefs change when something new shows old beliefs to be false.

For example, if an organisation has always tolerated people not working to policies and procedures, staff will believe that rule-breaking doesn't matter. However, if managers start to take disciplinary action when rules are broken and/or start to reward those who support policies, staff will start to believe that rule-breaking is not acceptable.

Changing culture means changing behaviour and beliefs as much as processes or structures. One of the most powerful symbols of change is the behaviour of the person leading or managing change. Their behaviour, what they say, and what people say about them, gives a powerful signal about what is appropriate behaviour during the change period, and afterwards.

3.3 Your organisation's current approach to change

The next sub-section examines some approaches to change that have been identified by researchers and writers about change. But before we do that, it's useful to consider your own organisation's current approach to managing change.

- What is your organisation's prevailing management style? Directive and controlling? Supportive and empowering? Trusting both leaders at the top and 'leaders' at the bottom?
- Is the organisation driven by a strong or weak leader? How often and to what levels of the organisation does the leader consult?
- Which elements of the organisation are kept at the top, and which are devolved downwards?
- Is information too liberally communicated, or kept secret, or is there a good balance?

To help you think about your organisation's current approach to managing change, ask yourself:

- Is it clear what's causing the change, what our approach to the situation actually is and what the end result of change will be?
- Is it clear who's leading change? Has that person or group set out a vision that others believe in and will work towards?
- Do people know specifically what is changing? Do they know how they might be affected? Have they been able to shape or define the change for themselves?
- Has the path towards our intended destination been clearly set out, and does everyone understand what part they play in making it a success?

Where does your organisation fit along these spectrums?

	1	2	3	4	5	6	7	
Clear								**Confusing**
Considered								**Chaotic**
Planned								**Reactive**
Inclusive								**Exclusive**
Open								**Secretive**
Trusting								**Suspicious**

3.4 Common approaches to change management

This section considers some common approaches used by other organisations to managing change, as identified by researchers into this topic. It outlines some of their benefits and drawbacks, and suggests when to use them. To help you decide whether a different approach might work for you, you could compare your organisation's current management style and current approach to change (perhaps using section 3.3 above) with these common approaches.

Participatory approaches may be more appropriate for incremental change. More involvement can help people to adapt to and own new ways of working and may ensure that change is more embedded in the organisation in the long-term.

More directive or controlling approaches are more appropriate where radical change is involved. In this scenario people often need to feel that someone is in control of the situation, and that lines of accountability and responsibility within the organisation are clear.

You may need to use a mixture of approaches within one change period. For example, the best initial response to a crisis in the organisation might be to adopt a directive approach. This deals with the immediate issues quickly and firmly and demonstrates clear leadership and control in a difficult situation. Once the situation is under control, a longer-term assessment of the situation can be made. A more participative approach can then be introduced to enable people to influence changes in the organisation.

The table opposite presents five different approaches to managing change.[7]

It describes each approach, its benefits and drawbacks and when it might best be used. The approaches are presented in order, with the most participatory first and the most directive last.

Look at the table opposite and consider which approach would best suit your organisation:

- at a time of stability
- at a time of slow but constant change
- at a time of wide ranging and rapid change
- during a crisis.

Approach	***Description***	***Means/Context***	***Benefits***	***Drawbacks***	***When to use it***
Collaboration/ participation	Involves those who will be affected by change in defining and planning change	People involved in setting strategy, agreeing action, resolving problems	Increased ownership of a decision or process May improve decision-making Increased commitment and future input	Time-consuming Can be difficult to manage diverse opinions	During incremental change or long-term transformational change
Education and communication	Involves the explanation of the reasons for and means of change	Communication assumes a vision and direction are established and that people trust their leaders	Overcomes lack of or mis-information Once persuaded people will often help implement the change	Time-consuming Direction or progress may be unclear	During incremental change or long-term transformational change
Intervention (or Facilitation)	Maintains co-ordination or control of change with a single person or group	Leader or change agent keeps control and delegates elements of change	Process is guided or controlled but involvement takes place	Risk of perceived manipulation	Incremental or non-crisis transformational change
Direction	Involves the use of managerial authority to establish the strategy for and means of change	Authority used to set the direction and means of change	Clarity and speed	Risk of lack of acceptance, or poorly thought out strategy	Transformational change
Coercion/edict	Involves the imposition of change or the issue of edicts about change	Open use of power through edict	Successful in a crisis or state of confusion	Least successful unless there's a crisis	Crisis situation; during rapid transformational change; change in an autocratic culture

Vision-based change

This is change that focuses on a vision of the future. The vision is typically centred on an outcome for users, but may also focus on outcomes for other stakeholders.

It is typically lead and championed by trustees/board members and senior management. Its management is often based on the underlying values and beliefs of the people involved in change.

7 Adapted from Johnson G and Scholdes K *Exploring Corporate Strategy* (Harlow, Pearson Education Ltd, 2002)

Chapter 4: Planning change

"One thing's for sure. If we keep doing what we're doing, we're going to keep getting what we're getting.

One definition of insanity is to keep doing the same thing and expect different results."

Stephen Covey, author of *The 7 Habits of Highly Effective People*

4.1 Why plan change?

As we have seen, there are many types of change, some planned and some unplanned. Even when the reason for change is originally unplanned, you will usually benefit from taking stock and planning a way forward. This chapter explores the practical issues you will need to consider when planning for change.

Good planning can mean the difference between successful change or failure. Planning for change involves stopping to think about what you want to achieve, focusing your time and resources on this goal. It can give staff a clear sense of what their role is and how it contributes to the goal. Finally, by encouraging you to anticipate potential problems in advance, planning helps to minimize mishaps.

4.2 What's involved in planning change?

Planning for change involves translating your vision of where you want the organisation to be into a more detailed plan of who will do what, when and how. The plan usually includes both the implementation of the change itself (e.g. introducing a new financial system or a new service) and the activities you'll undertake to help people deal with the change.

Consider carefully who you should involve in planning change, how and when. Involving key stakeholders can improve the plan and give them a stronger sense of ownership, but can also take longer and use more resources.

Don't make the mistake of thinking your change plan is set in stone. Change, by its very nature, is difficult to predict, so your plan will need to adapt to new challenges or opportunities that often emerge along the way.

As you adapt the plan, make sure the changes are highlighted to the right people, together with a brief explanation. If you don't do this, people may lose confidence in the process or think you're covering something up.

4.3 *The plan*

Your change plan might contain these headings:

- **Reason for change:** Why does the organisation need to change now? Has the need for change come from inside or outside the organisation? (See chapter 2)
- **Nature of change:** What is the scale of the change? What specifically will change and, importantly, what stays the same? Who or what will it affect? How quickly does this change need to happen? (See chapter 2)
- **Vision for change:** How will things be different afterwards? How will the organisation benefit? A compelling vision for change that people can understand and embrace will make managing change a far easier task.
- **Aims:** It helps to break down the vision into a handful of key elements. Be slightly more specific about what kind of changes you want to see and who will be affected.
- **Your approach to change:** Who will be involved in the process, when and how? (See chapter 3)
- **Key tasks:** What specific activities will need to happen in order to bring this change about?
- **Milestones:** Set some timed, significant steps towards achieving your aims. They should be perfect points at which to assess progress.
- **Budget:** How much resource you need, in cash and time.

Remember that a plan is only ever as good as the number of people that bother to read it, understand it and then put the plan into action. The plan doesn't need to be a long document. If it is, consider producing different versions to communicate the plan to staff and stakeholders. (See chapter 5 for more on communicating change.)

4.4 *Resourcing change*

Managing change is a challenging task, equivalent to managing an extra project or series of projects. Think carefully about what resources you will need to manage change effectively, including:

- money
- staff time
- staff skills, expertise and experience.

Include within your plan a budget identifying the activities and human resources needed during the period of change and costing them. To help you think about skills and capabilities to manage change, look at the roles and skills discussed in the section 'Building a team to support change' below.

Does your budget match your organisation's current resources? If not, can you get more resources through:

- money from a grant, your reserves, or some earned income?
- expertise from a consultant or a colleague in another organisation?
- training staff?
- recruiting more staff?

Budgeting for managing change is often difficult because change is hard to predict and may not go according to plan. A contingency fund, for both financial and time resources, can provide some flexibility to help you manage unplanned situations.

Building a team to support change

No one person can drive, support and manage change alone. It is important to build a core team of people who can work together with you to support change in your organisation. This team should ideally reflect or be able to tap into the views of key stakeholders and might include senior managers, trustees, project managers, external consultants and users. As with any team, a change team should also contain a good mix of skills, attitudes, perspectives and experiences. Finally, members of a change team can play different roles:

- Leaders
- Change managers
- Change agents
- Outsiders.

This may happen naturally, or you could try to make it happen by discussing about what these roles involve, and allocating them to members of your team.

> ***"Get a strong and balanced team around you, including your board."***
> **Project contributor**

Leaders

Successful change requires clear leadership. A leader is someone who:

- can create and convey a compelling vision for change;
- stakeholders can trust and follow through the time of change;
- ensures that the right changes are made and supported at the right time;
- embodies new and different ways of thinking and acting.

A change leader needs a number of key skills, including:

- the ability to cope with ambiguity;
- the ability to be flexible and adapt to the changing pace or nature of change;
- insight and sensitivity to the strategic and political context;
- the ability to relate to others and understand the needs of multiple stakeholders;
- the ability to manage change while maintaining current performance;
- the ability to be decisive at the right moments, and to have the authority to persuade others to accept these decisions.

A leader isn't necessarily someone at the top of the organisation. There may be people throughout the organisation providing leadership, such as a long-serving volunteer or staff member. Whether or not they have formal influence or authority, other colleagues look to them for leadership. These informal leaders are often vital in building support across a larger organisation. One way to do this is to give them a role in supporting change in the organisation.

It is also possible to view all your staff and volunteers as leaders – people with autonomy, with decision-making powers and ideas. They may not be leading the organisation, but most people are leading something. Organisations that encourage this devolved idea of leadership can find themselves much more nimble and able to move quickly when change happens, as people are trusted to make and implement decisions immediately without asking the permission of 'higher powers'. This relies, however, on a clear, well-understood, and detailed central vision. An organisation that has many leaders all leading it in different directions, or all managing change in 60 different ways at once, is clearly neither nimble nor fast-moving.

It is often said that there are two main types of leaders:

1. ***Charismatic or visionary leaders*** who are mainly concerned with building a vision for the organisation and energising people to achieve it. They are more often associated with managing change. Charismatic leaders are very valuable to organisations, but often they need to be supported by people who can implement and deliver the vision and strategy they set out. This support may be provided by a change manager.
2. ***Transactional or implementer leaders*** who focus on establishing systems and controlling the organisation's activities. They are more likely to be associated with improving the organisation from within.

Successful change needs both types of leadership, but it might not be provided by the same person. Different people might take on the 'visionary' and 'implementer' roles, working closely together. Both types are equally valuable in different contexts, and there is evidence that despite the obvious attractions of the charismatic leader, the quiet type can often create the most exciting, long-term, sustained changes.[8]

> ***Case study: Resourcing change***
>
> **Charity P3 created a specific management team to oversee its change. The team brought together operational, financial and HR managers to work alongside the chief executive and chair in dedicated planning and review of change activities.**

Change managers

The change manager is the person responsible for planning and delivering the change. They maintain the overview of the change tasks. They determine whether the change is going to plan, and put in place measures to correct things when they go wrong. The change manager may also be the leader.

Change agents

Change agents are individuals or groups that make change happen in an organisation. They are supporters and champions of change and are directly involved in implementing it. They may be the leader or change manager, but can also be senior or middle managers, trustees, junior staff, or even external stakeholders.

Outsiders

Although people inside the organisation have important roles to play, outsiders can also perform useful roles.

- *New managers:* Bringing in new managers during a time of change can increase the diversity of ideas and views in an organisation. Despite now being insiders, they can bring an external perspective and new skills and experience. They can help break down cultural barriers and act as a tangible signal of change. However, to be successful they need consistent and visible support from the chief executive or the board.

- *External stakeholders:* Your external stakeholders may include users[9], local and central government, the local community and the media. They are often key influencers, and may be respected by people inside the organisation. If they are briefed and involved properly, they can provide a powerful external reinforcement of change.
- *Consultants and advisers:* Consultants or outside experts can bring specific expertise or skills needed during the change period. They also bring an external perspective and signal symbolically the importance of the change to the organisation. You could use consultants as interim 'special project managers' or for discrete tasks such as facilitating a meeting with the change team. Consultants or experts should be used for clear and specific reasons and should not be leading the change.

Bear in mind that some third sector staff can be sceptical about using consultants or outside experts. They may fear that a consultant will not understand the context or culture of the organisation, or that managers may hide behind the consultant and use them to deliver any bad news, or even just that they are an expensive use of resources. Being careful how you introduce the consultant to the organisation can resolve some of these difficulties. A good consultant will be aware of them and will take steps to manage these issues.

4.5 Timing of change

It isn't always possible to choose when and how quickly change takes place. Sometimes you will be able to set the timescales yourself, but on other occasions outside factors will be in control.

Consider planning your timing to fit around:

- any other existing or planned changes – it may not be wise to try to implement too many changes all at once
- strategic or business planning cycles
- funding cycles.

If you have a choice, think carefully about what pace of change is desirable. Is it best to drive change forward as quickly as possible, or is it better to give people more time to prepare and deal with it? Should you move at the speed of the fastest, of the slowest, or of the majority?

Remember that the timing of outside factors can work for you, creating tactical opportunities. For example, a perceived crisis can be a great way to get buy-in to a change you've wanted to make for ages. A change that was planned but had no resources can be rapidly activated to fit through a suddenly opened window of opportunity.

Imagine that a competitor for your main contract with the local authority tries to move into the area. The chief executive might use this as the moment to resurrect and implement a plan to introduce a new outcomes monitoring system to help the organisation demonstrate what it achieves. People in the organisation will be more likely to accept the need for the new monitoring system because of the threat of real competition.

Case study: Ensuring long-term survival by working and planning together

After losing key contracts, the **North Somerset Enterprise Agency** needed to restructure its services to ensure its survival.

The Agency's board identified that the organisation needed to become more entrepreneurial in order to pursue new contract opportunities and be ready to take risks to secure its future. The board agreed to restructure its membership to include new members with a background and interest in generating income. After recruiting new members, the board led the development of a new strategic plan that re-defined the organisation's vision and purpose. The new strategic plan set the basis for a new business plan that set out clear goals, responsibilities and targets. Plans helped staff and board members alike to understand who and what was needed to achieve the goals set by the organisation.

8 Find out more about leadership at the Third Sector Leadership Centre **www.thirdsectorleadership.org.uk**

9 Mulelly J and Sturdy C *Centre Stage? Making Choices about Involving Users* (London, Performance Hub, 2008)

Project management

Project management tools that could be adapted for use in managing change include:

- *project summaries:* detailing objectives, milestones, key tasks, deadlines;
- *project plans:* detailing tasks, priorities, responsibilities, resources, organisation and individual stakeholder risks, and task dependencies;
- *project schedules or GANTT charts:* detailing sequence, timing and overlap of activities;
- *resource plans:* detailing what time, money, skills or expertise are required to complete certain tasks.[10]

Widescale or complex change may involve a number of projects to achieve one or more change objectives. This would involve the management of multiple related project plans.

Remember that change management is not the same as project management. Managing change can benefit from using project management tools and techniques, but in addition it requires a clear approach to engaging, supporting and managing people through clear leadership.

4.6 Understanding enablers and barriers

When planning change you may find it helpful to analyse your organisation's operating environment – that is, the things that are changing outside your organisation. There are a number of tools that can help with this:[11]

- an analysis of organisational strengths, weaknesses, opportunities and threats (SWOT analysis) to identify how and where the organisation needs to develop;
- an analysis of the political, economic, social, technological, legislative and environmental factors at play in the organisation's strategic environment (PESTLE analysis);
- an analysis of options open to the organisation as a route to achieving its goals (options appraisal);
- the creation of alternate future scenarios for the organisation, in which the likelihood of different scenarios is considered, the challenges and opportunities of different scenarios are identified and assumptions about the scenarios are defined and challenged (scenario analysis);
- a rating of the different positive and negative forces impacting upon your organisation (one version is known as 'forcefield analysis', see exercise on the right).

"Balance planning for change with the ability to flex and respond to changing circumstances along the way."

Project contributor

Exercise: Forcefield analysis

Your change plan might benefit from an analysis of the different positive and negative factors that are likely to affect it.

Forcefield analysis is a tool you can use to identify forces for and against the change so you can plan to make the most of the positives and minimise the negatives. It can be developed by the person responsible for planning change but is best discussed in a group.

Start by drawing up a table like the one shown in the example opposite and write in the forces you think might work for or against the change.

It is quite common for someone to suggest 'organisational culture' as a barrier to change. If this happens, think in a bit more detail about the elements covered under organisational culture in chapter 3, and see if you can identify specific elements of your culture that are barriers to change, and then check whether there are any cultural enablers of change.

Once your table is complete, rate how important each factor is, then discuss strategies for making the most of the positive forces, and keeping them going, while trying to find ways to reduce or work around the negative forces. Putting them all down in one place, and rating how important each one is, can help you to prioritise.

Example: Implementing a new IT system – Forcefield analysis

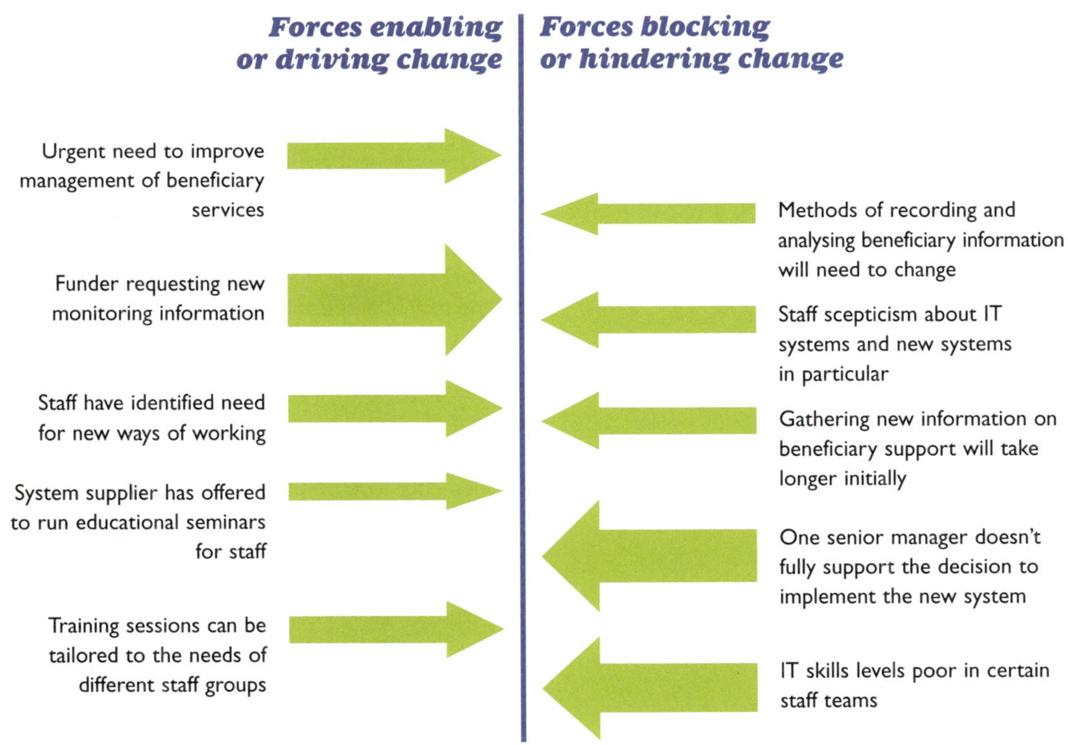

The width of each arrow represents the strength of the enabling and hindering forces. In the example above, the funder's request for new monitoring information is the most powerful driver for change, whilst the low levels of IT skills in certain staff teams is the biggest obstacle to overcome.

People

Managing change is often a complex and involved task, even *before* you start thinking about all the people involved! You may need to consider how your planned changes will affect all your stakeholders – the people, groups and organisations that have an interest in your organisation – and how they will affect the changes.

Internally you may need to think about staff, volunteers, managers, unions, members and trustees. Externally you may need to consider users and beneficiaries, funders, donors, other charities working in your field, government, your community, the media, and suppliers. Making sense of all these people can be tricky, so taking some time to understand their different interests and perspectives may give you some useful insight and suggest ways of getting at least some of these groups to lend you their support. Stakeholder mapping is a useful technique.

10 For a useful short introduction to project management and community used tools see the London Advice Services Alliance website at **www.lasa.org.uk**
See also **www.mindtools.com**

11 For more on these and other strategic planning tools see Copeman C and others *Tools for Tomorrow* (London, NCVO, 2004)

Exercise: **Stakeholder mapping**

Stakeholder mapping is a tool you can use to identify key stakeholders and consider both their interest in and influence over your organisation. It's best to do this exercise in a group.

The first step is to list all of your key stakeholders. Then draw up a matrix, plotting stakeholder interest and power. Through discussion, try to plot each of your stakeholders on the matrix.

This should suggest the approach you might take with each stakeholder, whether they need to be:

- managed closely
- kept informed
- kept satisfied or
- monitored.

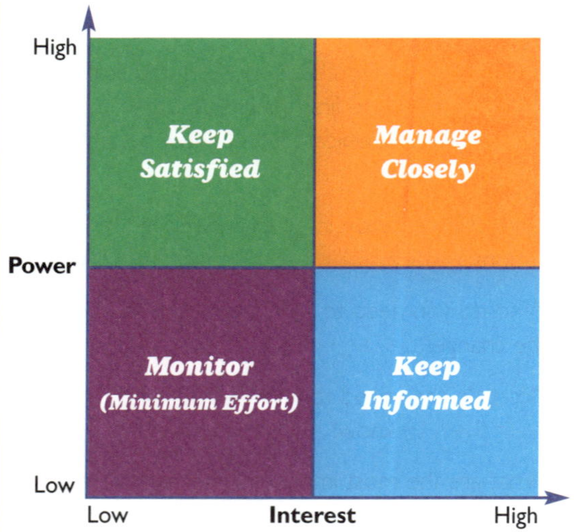

High interest, high power – manage closely

Stakeholders with the highest level of interest and power are those most able to assist with the change – or block it. Depending on the change, this might include funder partners or key managers and staff. Manage them closely by:

- engaging them early on to understand their position and perspectives on change;
- communicating with them in a variety of ways to ensure they understand, embrace and support change;
- involving them in change planning and implementation;
- supporting them to ensure their ongoing commitment.

Low power, high interest – keep informed

Stakeholders with little power but a great deal of interest in the change could create disruption by openly voicing dissatisfaction, which can in turn affect other groups. For example, it's not uncommon for administrative staff to be given little say in the re-design of working practices. However, it would be totally disruptive if these staff failed to use the new systems properly, or kept using the old systems, because they don't believe in the new systems. Keep these stakeholders informed by:

- communicating the vision and overall plan for change;
- involving them to plan and implement the change;
- communicating regularly on progress and achievements.

High power, low interest – keep satisfied

Stakeholders with a lot of power but little interest in the change can also help or hinder it. For example, a grant funder may have no direct interest in whether your performance management arrangements change, unless they suddenly start getting data in a new format. Give these stakeholders all the information they need in the format they prefer but be careful not to bother them too regularly.

Low power, low interest – monitor

Stakeholders with little power over or interest in the change may not appear to need a strategy for engagement. Be sure not to bother them with too much information. However it is worth maintaining an understanding of their position. Monitor their position by:

- communicating periodically on progress;
- giving them opportunities to comment on change.

Stakeholder mapping may highlight that an individual or group of stakeholders appears in the 'wrong' part of the matrix. To enable change to happen effectively that stakeholder needs to be more directly engaged and involved to ensure their support.

For example the trustee board might appear in the keep satisfied (high power, low interest) quadrant, whereas you feel your trustees should have a high interest in this change process and think they should be in the manage closely quadrant. You may need a trustee 'charm offensive' to engage them and generate their public support for the change.

Chapter 5: Communicating change

Well-managed communication is crucial to managing change successfully. It ensures that people inside and outside the organisation understand the changes you're making. Poor communication is the most commonly cited cause of complaint and failure in any area of organisational management.

5.1 Planning communications

Planning your communications involves deciding who needs to know what, when and in which format. A blanket approach to communications – the same message at the same time in the same format to everyone – is often wasteful and ineffective.

If you have a change team, ask them to help plan your communications. If your organisation has someone skilled in, or responsible for, internal and external communications, ask for their input.

Don't put off thinking about your communications. It should be one of the first things you do, so that you are ready to communicate with people before the change begins.

Good communication involves answering five key questions:

1. Who do you need to communicate with about the change?
2. What do they need to know – and what do you want them to know?
3. What are the most important messages for each stakeholder group? Try not to communicate more

Case study: Communicating change

Charity P3 used a variety of methods to share its plans for development with stakeholders. Staff participated in frequent one-to-one and group meetings. They received dedicated newsletters and got to know the organisation's newly adopted outcomes indicators through a programme of training. Trustee board members participated in regular focused board meetings, which were supplemented by regular review meetings between the chief executive and the chair.

than three key ideas in a single communication. Obviously, you will change these messages over time, especially if it's a long-term process.

4. What communication method best suits each stakeholder group and the kinds of messages you are communicating? Major news about redundancies, for example, should not be mentioned over the water cooler, or through a text message.
5. When do you need to communicate with each stakeholder group, and who will do this? Not everyone should know the same things at the same time. Staggering what you say often helps, first telling those most directly affected and then telling others. Don't forget to be clear who's telling who what – a badly implemented plan is as bad as no plan at all.

5.2 What to communicate

During a period of change, people will generally want to know what will change, when and how, how it affects them and what their role is.

The 5Ps of change communication[12] can help you decide key messages for each stakeholder group.

Purpose: Why do we have to do this?
Picture: What will it look like when we reach our goal?
Plan: How will we get there, step-by-step?
Part: What can (or must) I do to help us move forward?
Prize: What impact will the change will have on others (the organisation, individuals, users, partners)?

Example

Purpose: Our client case load has grown rapidly in the past 12 months. Recent feedback from line management reviews has highlighted that our paper-based client case notes and background are becoming unmanageable. We're implementing the new client case management system to help us better manage individual client records and support worker supervision.

Picture: With the new client case management system, and less paper to manage, we'll be able to supervise and deal with client case-related issues more quickly and easily. Communication within the team and with partner agencies will be improved, and admin reduced. We'll better support our clients and save time and resources.

Plan: We'll be consulting everyone on the introduction of the new system. The ICT-based software will be installed on everyone's PC within three months. A full programme of training and support will be provided. Paper-based records are being transferred to the new system within that period. We'll monitor use and performance of the new system for six months, and report back on its initial performance after three months.

Part: You can help shape the implementation and training plan by participating in our consultation workshops, and by commenting on plans via your line manager. Start talking to your line manager now about any practical issues about the transfer of client case records. Please also explain the new system and the reason we're introducing it to your clients. Further guidance on client briefing will be provided. Remember to highlight any issues or concerns about the new system as soon as they happen.

Prize: Spend less time managing paper and finding information, and more time with your clients.

5.3 How to communicate

Communications channels

Think about conveying messages using a mixture of the written and spoken word as people learn and remember information in different ways. Remember that action may be the most powerful medium of all. People will want to emulate the actions of those they admire and respect.

There are numerous forms of internal and external communication available to you.

Internal forms include:

- one-to-one meetings
- team or department meetings
- presentations or briefings
- interactive workshops
- email
- phone calls
- staff or volunteer newsletters
- board minutes
- intranets.

External communication channels include:

- newsletters
- events
- emails
- direct mail
- websites
- leaflets
- press releases.

Principles of good communication

When communicating remember:

- **Communicate regularly:** Plan regular updates throughout the change to reassure people. Plan specifically targeted communication to highlight or explain key activities, issues or achievements.
- **Be consistent:** Inconsistency creates confusion, tension or mistrust.
- **Keep it simple:** Convey a clear message using plain English and avoiding jargon.
- **Use images, metaphors, analogy and examples:** A descriptive picture or idea is worth a thousand words of rational explanation; it can get an idea across quickly and simply.
- **Use a variety of channels:** A mixture of meetings, emails, events, formal and informal occasions can all be used.
- **Don't be afraid to repeat yourself:** Ideas often only sink in after they've been heard many times.
- **Lead by example:** If influential people in the organisation start to adopt new systems or ways of working, others will follow suit.
- **Communication means dialogue:** Remember that communication should always be two-way. Make it clear how people can ask questions, comment or raise any concerns.
- **Be honest and transparent:** Be as honest as you can, but think carefully about timing.

More on honesty and transparency

It is vital to communicate honestly during a period of change. However, this does not mean telling everyone everything all of the time. You'll need to use your judgement to decide what to say, when and to whom. This can depend on the outcomes you want, the types of people and issues being discussed and the principles and values that are important to an individual and your organisation. For example, if a period of change may involve staff redundancy, it may not be possible to be entirely transparent about the potential outcome of legal advice, or the decisions that might be taken after a staff consultation.

You might want to be entirely open and transparent, but doing so may not be beneficial for everyone involved. It is usually sensible to avoid communicating dozens of small, detailed changes or steps in the process. People usually appreciate hearing that the process is happening, and will want to hear the final outcome, but don't necessarily benefit from getting hourly updates of the latest news.

Case study: Communication and consultation supports new management arrangements

Greenwich Housing Rights (GHR) was formed in 1984 as a housing advice and campaigning organisation in south London. Staff originally worked as a collective, sharing casework, project work and management responsibilities. However, as casework grew and became more complex over time, the trustees felt the organisation needed a more formal management structure to provide clearer leadership.

The trustees invested a lot of time in planning internal communications before making changes. GHR felt this was vital to minimising any conflict and stress caused by confusion during the change.

A joint working party of staff and trustees discussed and drafted options for staff management in 2005. In 2006, staff and trustees agreed to trial a new management structure, and to appoint an existing member of staff as a part-time manager. In 2007, staff voted to adopt this system.

During the trial period the acting manager was careful to communicate clearly in order to manage the concerns staff had about losing autonomy and independence in their areas of work. The manager drew up a 12-month management action plan, which was agreed by staff and trustees. Weekly staff meetings continued during the transition period and the manager reported on progress on a quarterly basis. Although the manager was given the decision-making powers previously held by the staff collective, staff were still consulted on key decisions. This consultation and communication slowed down decision-making but was vital to building trust in the manager and the system.

"Make things as simple as possible, but not more simple than they really are."
Albert Einstein

12 Adapted from the 4Ps model proposed by Bridges & Mitchell. Bridges W and Mitchell S 'Leading Transition: a new model for change', in Hesselbein F (ed) *On Leading Change: insights from the Drucker Foundation's journal* (San Fransisco, Jossey-Bass Books, 2002)

Chapter 6: Supporting people through change

"Get the right people in place around you - people you trust and who are skilled for the jobs you need doing."
Project contributor

People are *the* major influence on whether change in an organisation is successful. As we have seen, staff, trustees, funders, volunteers, users and partners can act as either enablers of or barriers to change.

This chapter explores people's reactions to change and what you can do to help them accept, deal with and adapt to new situations.

First we look at a couple of psychological models that you might find useful. Then we look at the issue of resistance, followed by an examination of the practical support that you can offer to people. We end with a look at you – the leader or change agent – and the support you need for yourself.

6.1 Understanding people's reaction to change

Change can be very stressful. People are often forced out of their comfort zone. Their world can go from being familiar, comfortable and predictable to unfamiliar, unsettling and unpredictable. Those not leading the change, can feel out-of-control and as if the change is being 'done to' them. They may react negatively if they fear that:

- their job is at risk;
- their role or working environment might change;
- they lack the skills or expertise needed for new systems or ways of working.

Others may embrace change, either because they're naturally stimulated by new things, or because they dislike the status quo and want particular changes for the organisation or for themselves.

Tool: The Kubler-Ross cycle

The diagram below highlights seven stages that people typically pass through during a period of change.[13] According to the theory, people only finally accept their situation after passing through each stage in turn.

The stages are:

1. **Immobilisation or shock:** Initial paralysis at hearing the bad news
2. **Denial:** Trying to avoid the inevitable
3. **Anger:** Frustrated outpouring of bottled-up emotion
4. **Bargaining:** Looking for a way out, seeking to negotiate a different outcome
5. **Depression:** Final realisation of the inevitable
6. **Testing:** Seeking realistic solutions
7. **Acceptance:** Finally finding the way forward.

The theory argues that, although there is no short-cut through the stages, people can be supported through each stage to help them accept change, and can be helped through the stages more quickly.

Only when people have moved to 'acceptance' can you realistically engage them in working with you to make the change happen. It's pointless to ask people to contribute to the organisation's thinking and planning when they're firmly in the denial or anger stages.

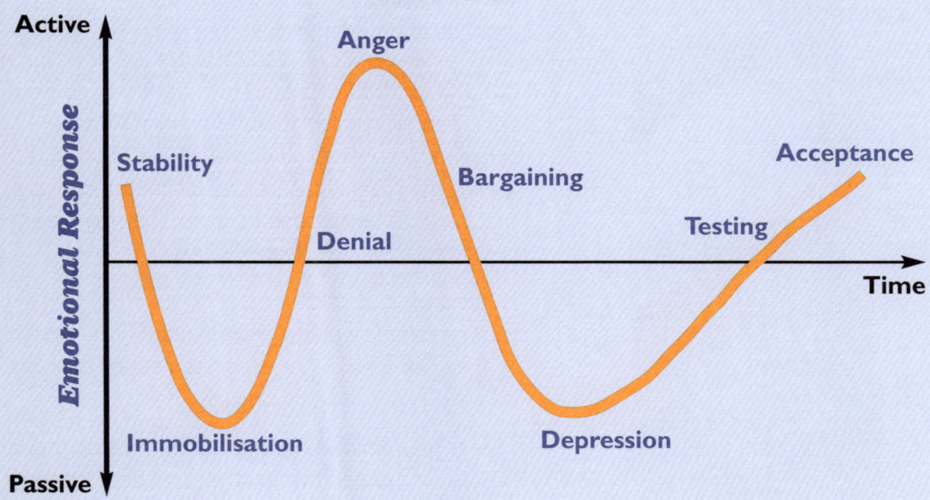

13 Elizabeth Kubler Ross studied the effects of bereavement in the 1950's. Her work was equated to 'bereavement at change', and has been adopted as an approach to anticipating and managing reaction and resistance to change.

6.2 *Dealing with resistance*

To deal with resistance, first you need to identify it. This is not always as easy as it sounds, as people express resistance in different ways. For example, people might:

- complain or voice concerns to managers or people outside the organisation;
- refuse to participate in group activities;
- refuse to adopt new ways of working;
- send emails criticising the planned changes;
- do nothing.

A stakeholder analysis can help you identify where resistance might lie and what form it might take (see page 20). To help you think about resistance to change ask yourself:

- How might the planned change appear to a frontline worker, a project manager or a founding trustee? Will it affect each differently?
- How might each resist your plans? What might they do? What might they say? Would they act openly or covertly?

'Organisational politics' is the way people in organisations exert power and influence over each other. Whether you like it or not, organisational politics *will* influence the way change takes hold in your organisation – your job is to manage this.

Support from influential people can help other people to accept the change. Lack of support, or open criticism, can seriously damage your plans. Consider whether you have allies or supporters inside or outside the organisation. They could be trustees, respected staff

members, or influential funders or partners. Engaging allies can help you overcome resistance, smooth relationships or champion the change.

You may have enemies as well as allies. Are there particular individuals or groups who will work to undermine the planned change? They may not act openly, but they can spread dissent, start rumours, or challenge the organisation in open meetings.

You can use a number of different approaches to deal with people offering resistance. They include:

- engaging them openly to help them understand and addressing their concerns or objections;
- using allies they trust or respect to help engage them;
- isolating them and working around them.

In some cases, it may not be possible to break down resistance or overcome opposition. The only options are to live with it and manage around it, or ask people to leave. If their resistance becomes severe, you may need to consider disciplinary action, potentially leading to dismissal. You should respect the legal and moral rights of your employees and ask yourself, "Do they have a point?" But if you have good evidence, do not be afraid of dealing directly, if fairly, with an employee who is damaging the organisation by failing in their role.

Before you embark on a change process, you should certainly consider whether you're going to get enough support from enough people. If no-one wants this change, and are unlikely to change their minds, then you'll be alone and will probably fail. Even if you succeed, what will be the costs to you and the organisation, and will the benefits be worth it?

Case study: Overcoming resistance

Following changes in Financial Services Authority rules, **Ipswich and Suffolk Credit Union Ltd (ISCU)** decided to extend its area of benefit to the whole of Suffolk. This meant a rethink of the way ISCU attracted new members and managed its local access sites.

ISCU identified local partners to help it develop local sites in new locations. At existing sites ISCU kept working arrangements as stable as possible. It continued to value small local teams that could support each other, while recruiting new teams in new areas. The board took a firm line in maintaining local ownership of volunteers and choices. This slowed ISCU's expansion but enabled it to retain a "large credit union, small friendly local team" approach.

6.3 Providing practical support

Practical support can help people adapt to new situations and overcome their initial resistance. It also demonstrates the organisation's commitment to its staff and volunteers, as well as its commitment to making change happen.

Some staff may need to re-learn or re-think their work if you alter their job role or reporting arrangements. Their performance might drop off slightly while they make personal adjustments. If a significant number of staff are affected in this way, the organisation will experience a dip in overall performance.

Staff and volunteers may need support to:

- learn new skills or ways of working;
- understand new working arrangements or services;
- talk openly about their feelings and experiences, either with colleagues and managers, or one-to-one with someone they trust.

Depending on the duration, scale and extent of change, a support programme might include:

Personal support

- training on specific skills relating to the change
- coaching on the job to supervise new ways of working
- mentoring from a trusted individual who can provide appropriate support and guidance
- counselling

Organisation-wide support

- online discussion forums (moderated by the organisation)
- intranet (or noticeboard) based 'Frequently asked questions' briefings

Adjustments to management

- temporary adjustment of contracted hours or responsibilities
- changes to performance management arrangements to reflect new ways of working.

Tool: *Unfreezing, moving and refreezing*

Kurt Lewin's model[14] assumes that, in order to change, people need to go through three stages:

1. Unfreezing
2. Moving
3. Re-freezing

The model is useful because it acknowledges that people need support to change. It assumes that things don't change overnight, and that ongoing encouragement and support is an important element in sustaining change for the long term. It recognises the need for periods of stability during change, through which people can re-build a sense of familiarity, comfort and ownership of the organisation and the activities around them.

This model can be used to help plan different types of support for people at different stages of the change process.

1. Unfreezing
Old ideals and processes must be given up so that new ones may be learned. People need support and encouragement to leave behind the familiar and break old habits.

2. Moving
New ideals are learned by doing. Coaching and support provided as people learn new ways of doing things. Recognition and reward for adopting new ideas.

3. Re-freezing
New ideals and ways of working are intellectually and emotionally accepted. Learning is practiced on the job. Support is given and achievements are celebrated.

Unfreezing tactics might include:

- visioning: using shared visions help people see the future;
- setting a challenge: "what's our solution to this problem?"
- providing evidence of the need to change;
- training to help people to learn how to do things differently;
- setting goals and targets to motivate people to achieve.

Moving tactics might include:

- highlighting change and ensuring everyone acknowledges it;
- facilitation to guide or provide focus in meetings or task groups;
- providing space and time for people to talk about their concerns;
- breaking things down into smaller elements to make them more manageable;
- joint planning and review, enabling people to work together on common issues.

Re-freezing tactics might include:

- removing old ways of working to ensure there's no way back;
- setting a new challenge to get people looking to the future: "how can we make this even better?"
- rewarding people for embracing new working practices;
- building change into formal systems and structures;
- building change into the social fabric of the organisation e.g. celebrating the results of change in staff meetings or public events.

14 Lewin K *Field theory in social science* (New York, Harper & Row, 1951)

Case study: Supporting staff through change

Aaina Asian Women's Group needed to ensure that its staff could manage the increasing number of projects being delivered by the organisation. The impact of new projects on staff training, supervision and personal development needs was not understood. Through its monitoring and reporting activities, Aaina had also identified that staff lacked effective line management support and guidance.

To support its future growth, Aaina helped staff identify their own training and support needs. It identified appropriate sources of training through contacts in the local area, and introduced managed supervision and review sessions with staff.

6.4 Supporting yourself: personal tools and strategies for change leaders

While you're supporting others through change, don't forget that you need support yourself. Leaders and managers in third sector organisations often say they feel isolated and unsupported in their role, particularly during times of change. You may have to drive forward new ways of working or thinking, ahead of the rest of the organisation.

Here are some practical personal support tools and strategies. You should have a good look at these and consider using one or more to create your own personal support system. Probably the most important is the final one in the list: finding a mentor or other person to talk to about change, sharing your concerns and sounding out new ideas.

Remember as a leader or manager you are not alone. Managing change successfully needs a team approach, as outlined in chapter 4. You should also consider contacting leaders in other organisations, who may have faced similar challenges to you. If you ever feel at your wits end, go for a walk or phone a friend.

"Get support, perhaps a mentor, at times of stress."
Project contributor

Write a journal or diary	Keep a journal of issues, activities, results and achievements over a period. It helps to organise your thoughts about the change situation and the way you're managing it. Even if you don't actively put words onto paper, simply reflecting on everyday occurrences helps to look at things differently. Consider how situations look from other people's viewpoint. If you were in their shoes, how would you feel about things?
Stay on top of it all	Set out a checklist of the key issues in managing change, and review the key issues fortnightly. Are you on top of them?
Manage your time	Personal and time management tools, such project plans, to-do lists, action points, diary reminders and regular review meetings play an important part in helping you stay on top on the situation.
Have a break	Try to take some time out to unwind and switch off outside of work. Doing something just for yourself, whether it's yoga, a game of football or reading a good book, will help concentrate your mind elsewhere so you can return to the change process refreshed. If all else fails, stop the change process for a few weeks and see how you feel about it then.
Find a team	Bring together a team that can share delegated responsibilities and support you and others.
Keep your distance	De-personalise the change you're managing. Take responsibility but distance yourself from sole accountability.
Stay positive	Staying positive helps others to do the same, and so makes managing them a more positive and productive experience. The vision at the end of the change should inspire you, not just your colleagues. Keeping a sense of humour can help you get through difficult times.
Keep it real	An objective perspective helps to maintain a rational and proportionate response to the situation. If you're faced with a difficult situation, try to step outside and ask yourself whether it will matter in a year's time.
Find a mentor	Having a neutral person to talk to who is outside the formal management structures of the organisation, and is not subject to the change you're managing, is a powerful support. Decide whether you purely need someone to listen, or whether you need someone to advise too. In the latter case, find someone who's already experienced in dealing with a similar situation.

Chapter 7: Sustaining change

"You're not alone. It's a team effort - you can't manage everything single-handedly."
Project contributor

Sustaining change can be really hard, particularly if the change takes place over an extended period or on many fronts. This is especially true if a leader or manager attempts to manage change single-handedly.

Over a long period, people can lose the energy and enthusiasm that was built up at the start of change. In this chapter we consider some of the challenges of sustaining change and some ideas for dealing with them.

7.1 Changing at a sustainable pace

Changing at a sustainable pace is an important but difficult discipline. Marathon runners learn quickly not to sprint off at top speed, but managers can struggle to learn this lesson. If you can maintain a sustainable pace of change it suggests that you are genuinely managing the change and not just reacting to things. You are giving people time to adapt to new situations while still keeping things moving.

Some changes happen faster than others. Understanding that the pace of change will vary at different times can help you prepare realistic plans and schedules for activity.

Change is often seen as a journey toward a destination, following a planned path. But the journey is unlikely to pass at a constant speed, or in a straight line. People don't react the same at every train or filling station, or cope with the length of the journey in a predictable and consistent manner.

Trying to accelerate the pace at the wrong time can create additional tensions or conflict. Acknowledging that the pace will vary can help you prepare realistic

plans that allow time to embed of new ways of working. This helps stakeholders feel comfortable that change is happening at an acceptable pace.

If the change doesn't happen at a sustainable or manageable pace, stress can increase and the success of the whole change process can be put at risk. This is because humans tend to be creatures of habit, and we will tend to revert to established practice when we can. Without support to help us adjust to new ways of working we'll go back to the comfort of the familiar and find ways to side-step the things we find difficult. The rest of this section offers a few ways of avoiding this.

7.2 Creating 'safe havens'

Change can feel relentless and exhausting. After a while, even change that is positive, exciting and creative can leave people feeling worn-out. Creating a 'safe haven' for people can help them to internalise and come to terms with change, experience some of the benefits, or recover and re-group before starting out on the next phase. A safe haven could take the form of:

- a period of time before implementing further change;
- retaining a system or practice from the past that represents familiarity and stability;
- a reflection event where people can come together to explore the benefit of change, share learning or difficulties.

7.3 Stress during change

Change creates stress, both for those driving it and those experiencing it. Some stress can be positive, and for some people it temporarily generates higher performance. But that is seldom sustained over a longer period or if the causes of stress increase.

You should make time to understand what effect change is having on the people around you, and on yourself. (See chapter 6 for ideas about supporting others and dealing with your own stress.)

7.4 Sustaining motivation during change

Sustaining energy, commitment and interest throughout the change is a challenging leadership role. People need support and encouragement on a regular basis to help deliver change.

You can help people stay motivated by:

- reinforcing the vision or reason for change;
- recognising and rewarding them for adopting new working practices;
- assessing progress, rewarding and celebrating achievements.

Reinforcing the vision

Regular briefings and communications, team meetings or away days, are useful ways of refreshing people's understanding of the reason for change and the end vision.

"The most important things a leader can bring to a changing organisation are passion, conviction, and confidence in others."

Rosabeth Moss Kanter
(Harvard Business School professor and respected writer on change management)

Encourage people to visualise life after change and share their ideas with you. This encourages positive thinking but also allows any potential concerns to be aired and discussed. Help people to understand what part they can play in achieving the vision.

Appreciate how far you've come

In the midst of change, it may be difficult to feel that the organisation is actually making progress, particularly if the change is longer-term and far-reaching. Without a sense of progress and achievement, stakeholders can start to lose interest.

Monitoring progress can help sustain commitment to change. You can monitor your progress by:

- looking at progress against the milestones in project plans;
- asking other people to review and validate your strategy and plan;
- carrying out surveys of the perceptions or experiences of change at different stages amongst different groups of people;
- running events to present the organisation's vision, strategy and progress through your plan for change, and gathering feedback;
- consulting people to assess their – and your – progress with the plan.

You should also make use of information from day-to-day activity, such as:

- feedback slots in management meetings
- staff supervision and appraisal meetings
- staffroom or office chat.

Take time to reflect on how far you've already come by remembering your starting point and revisiting major achievements.

Rewarding and celebrating progress

Acknowledging and celebrating progress helps to motivate people and overcome resistance during a period of change. It can help win people's enthusiasm and support during a potentially challenging period.

A simple way to acknowledge people is to thank them for their support and involvement. Or you could go a step further by making an announcement or throwing a party. If your achievements are particularly newsworthy, you could try to get the media interested.

Setting attainable, immediate goals ('quick wins') can be particularly helpful. A quick win could be something quite simple, such as putting plants in the reception area. Visible quick wins can encourage people to take the first steps towards different ways of working, or can show that change is possible and can make a difference. Planning some early quick wins can help people feel positive about change.

> ***"Congratulate yourself on what you've achieved - don't only concentrate on what still needs to be fixed."***
> **Project contributor**

7.5 Embedding change

Until new ways of working become the norm, people are likely to slip back into old ways of doing things. Change only truly embeds itself in an organisation when it becomes part of the culture.

Three things can help to embed change in an organisation's culture:

1. **Proving it:** Demonstrating how the results of change have helped improve performance.
2. **Role modelling:** Ensuring that managers and influential stakeholders personify the new approach. Their behaviour reinforces and sets the tone for the rest of the organisation.
3. **Persistence:** Using constant reinforcement to encourage changes in behaviour so that they become 'the culture'.

Some of the 'refreezing' techniques from the 'Unfreezing, Moving and Refreezing model' (see page 27) could help to embed change in the organisation's culture.

Recently some managers, and writers on organisational management, have called for the techniques and approaches used in managing change to be seen as part of everyday management. This is similar to the idea of the 'Learning Organisation'[15]. In a learning organisation, managers encourage and embrace the principle of continuous learning to the benefit of the organisation. A continually changing organisation might be one where:

- ➜ leaders continually revise and reinforce a vision focused on the user or beneficiary experience;
- ➜ leaders openly welcome and embrace new ideas as positive and beneficial;
- ➜ challenges or problems are openly shared, and people are encouraged to work together to find solutions;
- ➜ what's driving change or development, and how the organisation is responding, is regularly voiced and discussed, and future plans are developed through consultation and collaboration;
- ➜ people are rewarded for the results they've achieved, and the results are celebrated.

---

15 A Learning Organisation is defined as 'an organisation that learns and encourages learning among its people.' Find out more from the Chartered Institute of Personnel and Development at **www.cipd.org.uk**

Chapter 8: Solving problems along the way

"Balance planning for change with the ability to flex and respond to changing circumstances along the way."
Project contributor

Even the most comprehensively planned change can go in an undesirable or unexpected direction. Understanding potential problems can help you anticipate and manage these issues.

Every situation is different, but this chapter will help you understand some common problems, and what steps you can take to get back on track.

8.1 Solving common problems

Common problems include:

- ➜ Lack of strong leadership to guide the change
- ➜ Intentions aren't clear and understood
- ➜ People forget the purpose and focus only on the plan
- ➜ People misinterpret situations or make the wrong assumptions
- ➜ Hidden agendas, organisational politics, personalities and personal politics get in the way
- ➜ Valued staff are lost along the way
- ➜ Difficult situations aren't dealt with because of fear of conflict
- ➜ Leaders feel isolated and unsupported
- ➜ People's behaviour doesn't change.

The table opposite sets out what commonly goes wrong with change, and then offers suggestions to help you manage change successfully.[16]

Problem	*Suggestion*
Complacency. Trying to force change without taking everyone with you, and creating a sense of urgency about the change.	**Increase urgency.** Make the need to change clear and immediate. Inspire people to move, make objectives real and relevant.
No powerful guiding force. Major change needs endorsement from the top, supported by a group of other influential people in positions of authority.	**Build the guiding team.** Get the right people in place with the right emotional commitment, and the right mix of skills and levels.
Lack of vision. No compelling vision to direct, align and inspire people to achieve it.	**Get the vision right.** Get the change team involved in setting a vision that will inspire and motivate staff across the organisation.
Lack of communication of the vision. If staff and stakeholders are unclear what the change will achieve, they are unlikely to be motivated to change.	**Communicate for buy-in.** Tailor your communications to people's needs, keep the message clear and consistent and make sure people have a chance to ask questions.
Focusing on the plan, not the vision. The plan was only a means to achieving the end, but people have become focused on the plan, their tasks, and on systems, processes and timescales. Meanwhile, you're getting no closer to your vision.	**Revisit the vision.** Put the plan aside for a while and remind yourselves of the vision. Is it still relevant? Is it still worth aiming for? If so, reconsider the plan – is it still fit for purpose? If so, fine, but before you get started again, paint the vision again for your people – brighter, clearer, and sharper than ever.
People resist change. Staff or other stakeholders either fail to embrace change, or actively obstruct the process.	**Empower action.** Take time to understand people's concerns and provide appropriate support. Reward and recognise progress and achievements.
No short-term wins or benefits. If the change plan only focuses on ambitious, long-term changes, staff may lose motivation as they can't see progress being made.	**Prioritise some short-term wins.** Prioritising some short-term wins will help people feel that they're getting somewhere, and can achieve more. Sometimes small changes can make a big difference.
Declaring victory too soon. Being too eager to claim you've reached your goal before really knowing that the change you've made has stuck for good.	**Keep at it.** Foster and encourage determination and persistence. Encourage progress updates, highlighting milestones and targets reached.
Change is not embedded. People adopt new processes and ways of working at first, but soon slip back into old habits.	**Embed the change.** Reinforce the value of successful change. Weave change into the organisation's culture.

"Take a deep breath and make one step at a time."
Project contributor

16 Based on material taken from Kotter J *Leading Change* (Boston, Harvard Business School Press, 1996)

8.2 ***Handling a crisis***

Unexpected situations are bound to arise and can create stress and de-rail your plans for change. Understanding how to manage the situation can help you to keep control at a stressful time.

Some unexpected events, such as a fire or a media scandal may constitute a crisis. A crisis needs urgent attention and direct action to minimise its impact. Crisis management experts set out six critical success factors for responding to a crisis:

1. **Leadership:** Leaders need the following skills and attributes to manage a crisis successfully:
   - calm, empathetic communication skills
   - self-awareness
   - ability to prioritise, delegate and make tough choices.
2. **Speed of response:** If you respond quickly to a crisis, the chances of safe recovery will be greater, but only if there's an effective plan.
3. **Planned response:** Take stock of the situation. Gather intelligence from those involved. Formulate a plan. Task trusted individuals to provide support. Prioritise.
4. **Adequate resources:** Get the right support in place, such as expert advisers, trustees, trusted peers and counsellors.
5. **Compassionate response:** Consider how people are feeling and what they need. They are likely to need decisive leadership – a sense that someone's in control and that there's a plan of action.
6. **Excellent communications:** Decide what message needs to be conveyed immediately and in the longer-term. Think about the needs of different stakeholders.

Crises are never comfortable but they can't always be avoided. Be ready to recognise a crisis if it happens and take prompt action when it does. Use the six crisis success factors above to guide your organisation's response.

8.3 ***Sources of further help and support***

There is an online companion to this guide that sets out further reading and resources you might find useful. You can find it at:
www.performancehub.org.uk/managingchange

For a range of support on change management and other performance improvement approaches, try the Performance Hub's Support Finder at:
www.performancehub.org.uk/supportfinder

Remember that you're not alone in this change situation. We hope this guide has helped you to think about sources of organisational and personal support, and how you can access expertise, experience, wisdom and encouragement to make managing change a successful and positive experience.